Palm Trees

A Story in Photographs

PALM TREES
A Story in Photographs

David Leaser

Westwood Pacific Publishing

First published in the United States of America in 2005 by
Westwood Pacific Publishing
2021 Wilshire Blvd., Suite 200, Los Angeles, CA 90025
www.westwoodpacific.com

Front Cover: Cuban royal palms (Roystonea regia) *provide a picturesque
backdrop for a lake on the grounds of the Fairchild Tropical Botanic Garden in
Coral Gables, Florida.*

Page 1: The red fruit of a king palm (Archontophoenix cunninghamiana)
*glistens in the morning sun on a quiet street in Westwood, a suburb of Los
Angeles, California.*

Frontispiece: Coconut palms (Cocos nucifera) *line a saltwater lagoon in Hawaii.*

This page: A grouping of palms, including Drymophloeus subdistichus,
Neoveitchia storckii, Kentiopsis olivoformis *and* Veitchia arecina, *thrive in
Kaneohe, Hawaii on the windward coast of the island of Oahu.*

Publication Manager (United States): Tammy Guerra

Printed and bound in Korea by Daehan Printing

Cataloging-in-Publication Data

Leaser, David Eric.
        Palm trees : a story in photographs / by David Leaser.
        p.   cm.
        Includes bibliographical references (p.   ).
        ISBN 1-59588-010-0
        1. Palms. I. Title

635.9′77′45   2004103065

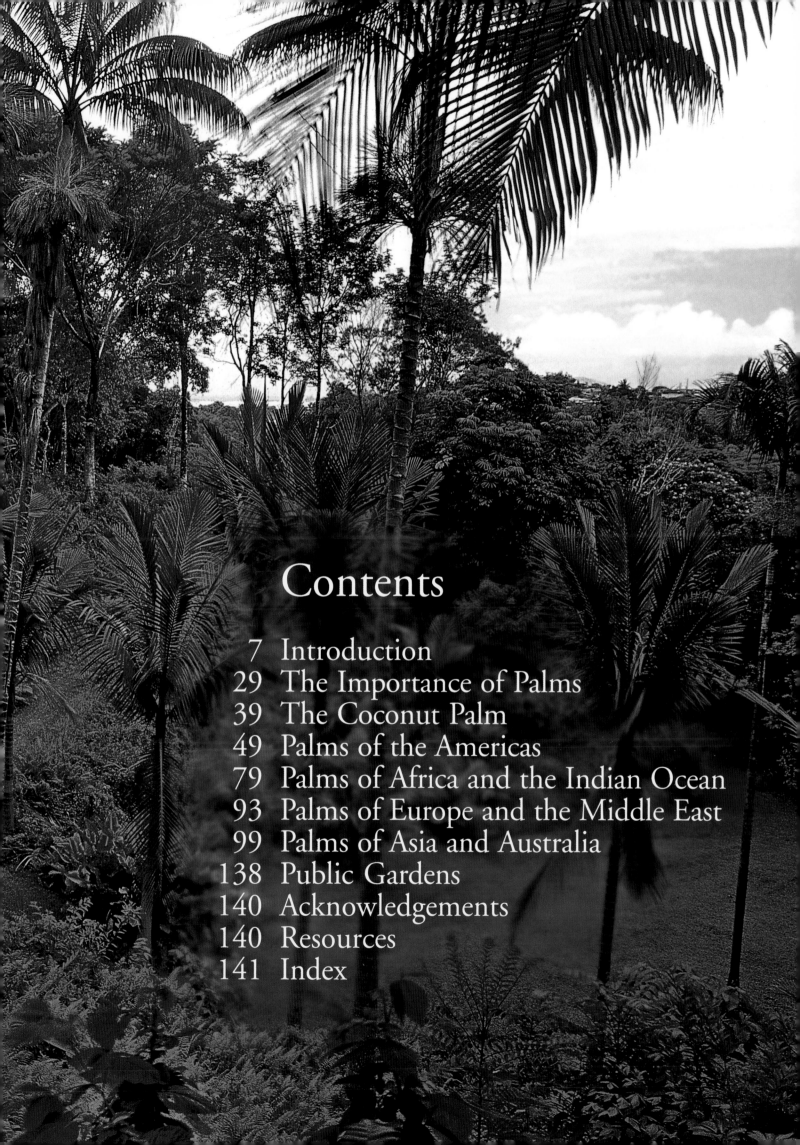

Contents

Introduction

It is hard to imagine a world without palm trees. The icons of the tropics, palms have played an important role in human civilization since the beginning of recorded time. Even our image of Eden is painted with tropical plants, flowers and palm trees.

The palm tree has always been the prince among tropical plants. In the 16th century, Swedish botanist Carolus Linnaeus, recognizing their importance to human life, labeled them Principes, the "princes" of the plant kingdom.

Indeed, palms are generally considered one of the most economically important plants in the world, second only to grasses. Throughout the tropics, entire towns and villages rely on palm trees for food, shelter and income.

Elsewhere, palm trees are valued for their sheer beauty and the inspiration they provide in the garden. In our minds, palm trees define the most beautiful areas of the subtropics and tropics. Picture Beverly Hills without its palm tree-lined streets, the Riviera without its stately date palms or the South Pacific without its palm-fringed beaches.

While palms have been a staple of life for centuries, the search for rare and exotic palms reached a frenzy in England during the 19th century. As its empire expanded, so did England's quest for rare and exotic plants. Wealthy plant collectors commissioned "plant hunters" to search the tropics for undiscovered palm trees, leading to the identification of a myriad of new species.

Above: The Palm House at Kew, built in the 1840s, still stands and is home to an outstanding collection of palms from around the world, including the tallest greenhouse-grown Chilean wine palm (Jubaea chilensis). *This illustration first appeared in the* Illustrated London News *in 1852.*

Opposite: The Bismark palm (Bismarkia nobilis) *is a striking blue-grey fan palm from Madagascar. Named for Otto Von Bismark, this palm is an ideal specimen for sunny subtropical climates. This photo was taken at the Fairchild Tropical Botanic Garden in Coral Gables, outside Miami, Florida.*

Above: In the 19th century, a massive Victorian greenhouse was imported from Europe and assembled in Golden Gate Park in San Francisco, California. The site quickly became a popular gathering spot for leisure-time activities. This photo was taken shortly after the glasshouse was erected in 1878. A young Canary Island date palm (Phoenix canariensis) *was planted at its entrance, and modern-day visitors to San Francisco can see the mature specimen standing next to the newly restored structure.*

Opposite: The coconut palm (Cocos nucifera) *adds grace and romance to any tropical setting. This specimen grows in the black sand of Punuluu Beach on the Big Island of Hawaii.*

Following spread: The shade of a blue latan palm (Latania loddigesii) *provides an ideal respite from the hot sun. Latan palms are slow-growing tropical trees and are nearly extinct in their native habitat on the Mascarene Islands because of development.*

Back in England, these palm trees were housed in elaborate greenhouses, or "conservatories." After a prohibitive tax on glass was repealed in 1845, thousands of glasshouses were constructed throughout England.

The most famous of these was the massive Palm House at Kew, built by Decimus Burton between 1844 and 1848. The structure, which still stands, measured more than 24,000 square feet and could display even the tallest palm specimens.

An even larger greenhouse was erected in 1840. The Great Conservatory at Chatsworth, designed by Joseph Paxton, was the largest of its day. The building was designed to allow Queen Victoria to ride through on a horse-driven carriage.

But perhaps the most important greenhouse developed in England was its smallest. In 1827, London physician Nathaniel Ward inadvertently invented the Wardian Case. After discarding a sealed glass jar, he noticed a small fern growing inside, nurtured by a small piece of mold and the water of condensation.

The Wardian case revolutionized plant distribution, allowing plant collectors to transport small palms and other exotics on long journeys through harsh conditions. When they arrived at their destination, the plants were in perfect condition.

The experiments and the determination of the early English plant collectors played significant roles in modern palm horticulture. Today, more than 2,500 species have been identified from the farthest reaches of the warm temperate to tropical worlds.

Opposite: The Canary Island date palm (Phoenix canariensis) *is ubiquitous in Mediterranean climates all over the world, including the Riviera and Southern California. These palms are relatively cold tolerant, growing as far north as Great Britain. This avenue of palms lines a path outside Westwood, a suburb of Los Angeles, California.*

Top: The Casbah in Morocco looks like a desert oasis surrounded by date palms (Phoenix dactylifera). *Many palms produce dates, but the true date palm, which may have been an ancient cultivated hybrid, produces the edible dates available for purchase in food markets.*

Following spread: This lake at the Los Angeles County Arboretum and Botanic Garden was made famous by the popular television show, "Fantasy Island." Because of it subtropical climate and large number of palm trees, Los Angeles often doubles in films for tropical locales. The three palm tree species shown here are the most commonly planted palms in California. Tall Mexican fan palms (Washingtonia robusta) *tower over the streets of Los Angeles. Canary Island date palms* (Phoenix canariensis), *like the one which leans over the lake, add a stunning focal point to a large garden, and queen palms* (Syagrus romanzioffianum) *form the staple for many palm gardens.*

Above: The Huntington Library, Art Collections, and Botanical Gardens in Los Angeles houses one of the best collections of subtropical palms in the world. At the center of the photo is an excellent example of a weeping cabbage palm (Livistona decipiens) *from Australia. To the left, smaller pygmy date palms* (Phoenix roebelinii) *from Laos make ideal specimens for smaller gardens. In the foreground, a Mediterranean fan palm* (Chamaerops humilis) *cultivar called "green mound" creates a nice accent. Mediterranean fan palms are cold hardy and can sustain frosts and occasional freezes.*

Opposite: Palm trees make outstanding avenue plantings, as demonstrated by this group of royal palms lining a path at the Fairchild Tropical Botanic Garden in Coral Gables, Florida. Two species of royal palm are represented here: Cuban royal palms (Roystonea regia) *line the left side of the path, while a more upright Venezuelan royal palm* (Roystonea oleracea) *stands to the right.*

Following spread: The stunning blue color of the blue hesper palm (Brahea armata) *makes an attractive accent in a desert landscape. Blue hesper palms are extremely drought- and cold- tolerant, making them ideal trees for warm temperate locations. Native to Mexico, these palms grow in rocky canyons with very little soil or water. This specimen was photographed in a desert garden at the former home of Henry Huntington. Huntington began developing a botanical garden in 1903, including a vast collection of rare and exotic palms. Now the Huntington Library, Art Collections, and Botanical Gardens outside Los Angeles, the palm collection is among the finest in California.*

Top left: The sabal palm (Sabal palmetto) *is native to the southeast United States, where it is prized as a landscape specimen. This palm is also called the cabbage palm because of its edible heart, or "cabbage." Unfortunately, the practice of destroying these palms for their cabbage has dramatically reduced their numbers in the wild. Sabal palms are drought- and salt-tolerant, as evidenced by this healthy grouping by the bay in Sarasota, Florida.*

Bottom left: The lattice effect of a trimmed Panama hat palm (Sabal causiara) *makes an interesting conversation topic in the garden. Called "boots," these leaf bases often support ferns and orchids in their native habitat, which ranges from southern North America through South America. While the modern landscape practice is to skin the leaf bases clean from the trunk, many prefer the interesting texture the leaf bases offer. This specimen grows in the Marie Selby Arboretum outside Sarasota, Florida.*

Opposite: Tall Mexican fan palms (Washingtonia robusta) *seem perfectly in scale at Hearst Castle in San Simeon, California. Mexican fan palms are the most common palms in California and are native to Mexico. In fact, these palms grow like weeds in most warm coastal areas, sprouting up in lawns and garden beds. Many avenues were planted with Mexican fan palms in the early 20th century, and these majestic trees still tower over many of California's cities.*

Following spread: The betel nut palm (Areca catechu) *is commonly planted in tropical areas for their seeds, which are used as a mild narcotic or stimulant. This grove of trees stands in a sea of maile-scented ferns at the Alii Marketplace on the Kona Coast of the Big Island of Hawaii. A screw pine* (Pandanus) *grows to the right.*

Opposite: California's seaside town of Santa Barbara provides an ideal climate for a wide variety of subtropical palms. Throughout town, palm lovers can see mature specimens of rare and unusual palms, some of which were planted nearly a century ago. The Santa Barbara Courthouse displays many fine palms, including blue hesper palms *(Brahea armata),* Chilean wine palms *(Jubaea chilensis),* paurotis palms *(Acoelorrhaphe wrightii),* Canary Island date palms *(Phoenix canariensis)* and Senegal date palms *(Phoenix reclinata).*

Above: Many palms are armed with sharp spines to protect them from grazing animals. This petiole of a Livistona *is lined with spines that would prevent even small birds from landing in its canopy. Spines such as these limit the landscape potential for many beautiful palms.*

Following spread: The gardens of Versailles, originally designed by Jules Hardouin-Mansart for Louis XIV, provide a stunning backdrop for dozens of container-grown date palms, which can be moved indoors during inclement weather. Similarly, palm enthusiasts in cold climates can over-winter frost-tender palms indoors and display them as container specimens during warmer months.

The Importance of Palms

Perhaps no plant plays a more significant role in civilization than the palm tree. In many tropical countries, palm trees are an economic staple, providing thousands of products from food sources to building materials.

Nearly every part of the palm tree can be put to use. Besides its obvious use as a source of lumber, the trunk of the palm can provide sugar, starch, vinegar and wine. Rattan is produced from the slender vine-like trunks of the rattan palms (*Calamus* and related groups), and walking sticks can be fashioned from the trunks of the lady palms (*Rhapis* species).

Palm leaves can be used as a source of food and animal fodder. Roofs can be fashioned from the thatch of palm leaves, and twine can be woven from the leaves of the raffia palm. Shoes, hats and other clothing items can be produced from palm fronds.

In some countries, natives prepare and eat palm flowers as candy. Palm flowers provide pollen and nectar for bees, which in turn produce honey.

The fruit of the palm provides a wide variety of uses. Many palms, like the coconut, date and peach palms, provide a variety of food choices.

Coir, the fibrous protective coating of the coconut, can be used for everything from carpet to insulation. Palm fruit is also an important source of oil, medicine and animal fodder.

Even the roots of the palm can be used in medicines or as a source of fiber.

Above: A man drinks from a coconut on the beach in the Trobriand Islands of New Guinea. Around the world, entire communities rely on palms trees for their survival. Coconut palms have many uses, from food staples to building materials. New cultivars grow smaller and bear more fruit than their ancestors, increasing the production of today's coconut plantations.

Opposite: The African oil palm (Elaeis guineensis) *produces one of the most important vegetable oils in the world. Today, millions of oil palms are grown in tropical plantations, creating one of the biggest export crops for many tropical countries. Today's genetically engineered oil palms produce larger fruit at an earlier age than their ancestors. This specimen grows near a red dirt road on the Hawaiian island of Kauai.*

Opposite: Coconut plantations can be found in nearly every tropical nation. Here, in Thailand, local women earn a living harvesting coconut fruit. Around the world, plantations of date palms, oil palms and betel nut palms provide food, shelter and income for entire countries.

Top right: These young boys partake in the coconut harvest in their native Western Samoa. Many coconut plantations grow a special cultivar know as the "Samoan coconut" which produces a much shorter tree. Its small size, plus its ability to produce fruit at a younger age, makes it an ideal tree for agriculture.

Bottom right: Palm trees serve many uses, including building construction. Leaves are used for roofing, trunks are used for timber and fibers are used for rope. This decorative ceiling in Fiji is made entirely out of palm-related products. Intricate designs are created by dying the fibers different colors.

Following spread: Palm-thatched roofs are common in tropical villages. This bungalow serves as a gathering place at the Ohana Keahou Resort on the Big Island of Hawaii. The Big Island is home to many carefully reconstructed examples of ancient Polynesian and Hawaiian architecture.

Top: In addition to their economic importance, palm trees provide an important element in the landscape. These majestic royal palms (Roystonea oleracea) *line a quiet street near Capesterre-Belle-Eau, Guadelupe. These trees provide shade and wind protection for travelers who bicycle and walk to work.*

Opposite: Palms make an ideal poolside planting. They are tidy and grow to a predictable size. Here, coconut palms (Cocos nucifera) *and pygmy date palms* (Phoenix roebelinii) *frame a fantasy pool at the Maui Marriott at Kaanapali.*

Following spread: Palms make outstanding landscape plants because of their beauty, easy care and predictable growth patterns. Palms of various sizes and colors can be used effectively to provide year-round interest. The Santa Barbara Courthouse in Santa Barbara, California displays the various shapes and sizes of many subtropical palms, including (from left to right) a Canary Island date palm (Phoenix canariensis), *clumping Senegal date palms* (Phoenix reclinata), *a shaving brush palm* (Rhopalostylis sapida), *more date palms, Senegal date palms and a stand of tall kentia palms* (Howea forsteriana).

The Coconut Palm

Nothing conjures up an image of the tropics like the coconut palm (*Cocos nucifera*). Its tall, arching trunk and elegant fronds add serenity to any tropical scene. The name *cocos* is derived from the Portuguese word for monkey, so named because of the face-like impression on the coconut.

Coconut palms have been cultivated for centuries, and remnant plantations exist throughout the world. Marco Polo wrote of them during his travels by boat to Sumatra in the 13th century. And even before that, Buddhists in Java carved bas-relief drawings in temples depicting coconut palms.

On the Hawaiian island of Molokai, descendants of King Kamehameha's royal coconut grove, planted centuries ago, still dot the north shore of the island.

Coconut palms are found in nearly every tropical location in the world, so much so that their origin is uncertain. Most botanists believe the coconut palm originated in Malaysia. Early explorers carried coconuts to the far reaches of the tropical world.

Today, coconut palms are among the most economically important plants in the world. Throughout the tropics, near one-half million people depend solely on the coconut for their existence.

Opposite: A coconut washes ashore on a sandy beach and begins to take root. Coconuts can survive and maintain viability for months before germination. The coconut will provide the moisture and nourishment the tree needs for its early development. As they root, coconut palms begin to tap into underground fresh or brackish water, allowing them to grow in the dry tropics.

Above: Entire islands have become inhabited by coconuts which wash ashore. These trees in Hawaii, however, were planted. Early Polynesians brought the first coconuts to Hawaii, adding beauty and value to the islands. This photo was taken at the Hawaii Tropical Botanical Garden outside Hilo on the Big Island.

Nearly every part of the coconut can be harvested. The coconut flesh, of course, is a source of food. And the coconut water, called coco frio, makes a thirst-quenching drink. During World War II, this coconut water was used in Japanese and American hospitals as a blood substitute for transfusions.

The tender flesh can be pressed and pounded to produce coconut milk. When dried, the white flesh, called copra, can be pressed to produce cooking oil, soap, cosmetics and margarine. Nothing goes to waste; leftover residue can be used as animal fodder.

In many tropical locations, entire villages are built out of coconut palms. Coconut trunks provide a sturdy framework for a house that will be thatched with palm fronds. Walls will be erected using leaf stems, and mats and baskets will be woven from the fronds. Rope will be fashioned from the palm nut's fiber, called coir, which can also provide insulation.

Many varieties are grown today. Some soar to more that 100 feet (30 meters) tall; others are smaller and more suited for the garden.

The coconut palm is undoubtedly one of the most important trees in the world. Its importance to civilization and its stunning beauty make it unsurpassed in the world of palms.

Top: A woman weaves a coconut rope in Zanzibar. Until recently, coconut rope production was the only economically important craft in the village.

Above: Vendors around the world prepare food products made from coconuts. These decorative drinks with pink lotus flowers are sold along the riverfront in Phnom Pehn in Cambodia.

Opposite: Many varieties of coconut palms have been bred for plantation use. These dwarf Malayan coconut palms allow farmers to easily harvest the crop. Taller trees require extensive labor as workers must climb the trees to collect the fruit. Photographed at the Fairchild Tropical Botanic Garden near Miami, Florida.

Following spread: Tall coconut palms prepare for a brief storm on the Big Island of Hawaii. These elegant trees can often sustain hurricane-level winds with little damage. High winds will defoliate the tree, but new fronds will quickly replace the damaged leaves. The palms in this photograph are located at the City of Refuge in South Kona on the Big Island of Hawaii. The City of Refuge was a sanctuary for prisoners and sentenced criminals on the run. Large stone walls, built centuries ago, still outline the city. The coconut palms in this photograph may be descendants of trees planted by early Polynesians in the mid-20th century.

Opposite: Coconut palms frame a black sand beach near the South Point of the Big Island of Hawaii. In addition to their obvious aesthetic and tropical appeal, coconut palms provide an important benefit to the beach: the roots help anchor the sand, enabling the beach to sustain strong winds and high surf.

Top right: A Rhesus monkey eats a coconut on Ko Samiu Island. Tame Rhesus monkeys have been trained to scale the large coconut trees and collect the harvest, reducing labor costs and danger for plantation workers.

Bottom right: This coconut palm has suffered severe trunk damage, giving it a corkscrew appearance. Yet the tree survives and provides a novelty attraction at a golf course on the Big Island of Hawaii. Palms trees can often sustain damage to their trunks and roots but grow into healthy specimens. If the heart of the palm, located where the fronds meet the trunk, is damaged, the tree will likely decline and eventually succumb to the damage.

Following spread: Coconut palms provide an idyllic backdrop for a tropical sunset.

Palms of the Americas

From the palm-lined streets of Beverly Hills to the thatched huts of Amazonia, palms play a significant role in the lives of Americans. They define the quintessential image of California, a landscape where palms provide the backdrop for nearly every setting.

As important as they are as landscape specimens, palms provide the livelihood for Americans living south of the equator. In the Amazon, families live in homes built from palm stems. Roofs are thatched with fronds and hammocks are woven from palm fibers.

Although the majority of the palms in the Americas grow in the tropics, some thrive as far north as New Jersey and as far south as Chile. The stately Chilean wine palm, now endangered, is considered by many to be one of the most beautiful palms in the world.

Opposite: Named in honor of Roy Stone, a 19th-century engineer in the United States Army, the Roystonea *genus contains some of the most beautiful palms in tropical America. They are characterized by their silvery gray trunks and prominent green crownshafts, the smooth area below the fronds at the top of the trunk. All make spectacular avenue plantings.* Roystonea princeps, *native to southern Jamaica, bears a nearly iridescent green crownshaft topped by elegant plumose fronds.*

*Above: The bright red fruit of the bamboo palm (*Chamaedorea microspadix*) is an added bonus to a beautiful landscape palm. Native to Mexico, this palm is one of the so-called "bamboo palms" because of its narrow, reed-like trunks and clumping nature. Valuable as landscape palms,* Chamaedorea *palms are perhaps even more useful as container plants for indoor use.* Chamaedorea elegans, *also known as "neanthe belle," is one of the most commonly grown houseplants in the world.*

Top left: The pindo palm (Butia capitata) bears stunning silver-grey to green fronds, making it an ideal landscape palm for warm temperate and subtropical climates. Native to Brazil, this palm is one of the hardiest in the world, able to sustain temperatures below freezing and periods of extreme drought. The pindo palm bears sweet, edible fruit which some say tastes like a mixture of peach, melon and mango.

Bottom left: Another strain of the pindo palm (Butia capitata), this version is called "strictior" because of its upright fronds. Pindo palms are highly variable; some have bright green fronds while others are light blue gray.

Opposite: The Chilean wine palm (Jubaea chilensis) is considered one of the most beautiful palms in the world. Named for King Juba, ancient king of what is now Algeria, the palm is native to a small area of Chile, where it grows in the dry savannah. This palm favors a Mediterranean climate with cool, dry air. The palm's massive trunk bears a treasure that has led to its demise: thousands of trees have been felled for its copious sap which produces an excellent wine when fermented. Nearly extinct, the palm is now protected in Chile, where efforts are under way to reforest the country. The palm bears a small seed which looks and tastes like a miniature coconut.

Opposite: Mexican fan palms line the paths of a park overlooking the Pacific Ocean in Santa Monica, California. These tall palms fare well with the salty, somewhat dry conditions of coastal California. They naturally maintain their dead fronds, giving them a petticoat appearance. In cultivation, however, most landscapers prefer to "skin" the palms to give the trunks a cleaner look.

Top right: The Mexican fan palm (Washingtonia robusta) *is an important feature in the California landscape. The genus, which contains two species, is named in honor of George Washington, first U.S. President. Native to Mexico, these tall palms are the most common palms in California and are also commonly planted in Europe and the Middle East. The beaches and streets of Southern California are lined with Mexican fan palms, as is this famous stretch of strand outside Los Angeles.*

Bottom right: California fan palms (Washingtonia filifera) *are indigenous to California, Arizona and Mexico, where they grow along stream beds. Able to survive in extremely arid conditions, these palms are ideal for dry climates. Featured here, Palm Canyon outside Palm Springs, California is one of the most beautiful places to see these palms in their native habitat.*

Following spread: California fan palms (Washingtonia filifera) *can survive severe weather conditions, including occasional fires. The chaparral in California burns on a regular basis, rejuvenating the native plants that thrive on the aftereffects. California fan palms have a thick, fibrous trunk that allows them to weather the firestorms. These palms in Palm Canyon near Palm Springs, California bear the scars of repeated fires, yet their beauty is unmistakable.*

Opposite: The Panama hat palm (Sabal causiara) is one of most stately of the sabal palms. Native to tropical and subtropical America, sabal palms are ideal for landscapes. Most are drought-hardy and some are among the most cold-tolerant of all palms. Panama hat palms can survive temperatures well below freezing. The specimen in this photo grows in the Marie Selby Botanical Garden in Sarasota, Florida.

Top right: The Texas palmetto (Sabal mexicana) is extremely drought-tolerant and an ideal palm for subtropical climates. Native to Texas through Central America, the Texas palmetto once lined parts of the Rio Grande River. Its habitat has been severely reduced because of human encroachment and agriculture. Texas palmettos grow in many botanical gardens and parks, including this palm on Sunset Boulevard in Beverly Hills, California.

Bottom right: The Hispaniola palmetto palm (Sabal domingensis) is similar in appearance to the Panama hat palm, but its fronds are somewhat bluish. These palms are native to the savannahs of Cuba and Hispaniola, but they are common in the Caribbean. This grouping grows on St. John in the U.S. Virgin Islands.

Following spread: The habitat of the sabal palm (Sabal palmetto) ranges from North Carolina in the United States through Cuba. Once common in Florida, its numbers have been reduced by poachers who sell the mature trees to landscapers. Also called the cabbage palm, this beautiful tree was once heavily harvested for its edible leaf-producing bud, which tastes like raw cabbage. Early Floridians picnicked near rivers, where they would chop down a palm and make a "swamp-cabbage" salad. Myakka River State Park in Sarasota, Florida is an excellent place to see mature specimens of various sabal palms in their native habitat.

Top left: The Cuban petticoat palm (Copernicia macroglossa) *looks more like a yucca than a palm. Its persistent leaves make this tree an interesting conversation piece in the landscape. Growing to about 15 feet (five meters) tall, this palm is ideal for small gardens. It looks equally attractive as a focal point in a tropical or cactus garden. Native to the savannahs of Cuba, where it grows in salt marshes, this specimen is at the Fairchild Tropical Botanic Garden outside Miami. The Fairchild features an outstanding collection of* Copernicia *palms.*

Bottom left: The bluish leaves of Copernicia hospita *are coated with wax, similar to the wax produced by its sister species, the carnauba wax palm (Carnauba prunifera). Although synthetic products have largely replaced it, carnauba wax is still refined from these palms in Brazil and used for a variety of purposes, including car wax.*

Opposite. The Bailey fan palm (Copernicia baileyana) *makes a stunning accent in the garden. Its massive size and concrete-like trunks add structure and a sense of permanence to the landscape. In its native habitat, it grows to 60 feet (18 meters) tall with a two-foot (.7 meter) diameter trunk. Named for famous horticulturist Liberty Bailey, this palm, like its family members, can tolerate occasional droughts, poor soil and seashore conditions.*

Opposite: The Syagrus *genus includes some of the most useful palms for the landscape. Native to South America and the Antilles, these palms are related to coconut palms, but are more cold hardy.* Syagrus sancona *is the tallest of the genus and reaches heights of 100 feet (30 meters). With its smooth grey trunk and long, arching fronds, this palm makes a stunning accent for large gardens. The Fairchild Tropical Botanic Garden near Miami, Florida displays a wide variety of* Syagrus *palms.*

*Top right: The queen palm (*Syagrus romanzioffianum*) is the most commonly planted palm in the genus. Native to South America, this palm is a popular landscape tree in subtropical climates because of its rapid growth and cold hardiness. Once established, this palm can grow more than two feet (.7 meters) per year. Queen palms are extremely popular in Southern California, where they are used to line avenues and driveways. In their native habitat, queen palms have many uses. Trunks are used to construct saltwater piers, leaves are fed to cattle and seeds are ground and fed to chickens. This specimen grows in the palm garden at the Huntington Library, Art Collections, and Botanical Gardens near Los Angeles, California.*

Bottom right: Although some palms branch, this queen palm at the Gizella Kopsick Palm Arboretum in St. Petersburg, Florida is an anomaly. The two-acre park features more than 300 palms, representing 73 species.

Top Left: The saw palmetto (Serenoa repens) grows in the coastal areas of the southeastern United States, where large stands cover sand dunes and act as an understorey for pine trees. Saw palmetto fruit produces a chemical in its fruit that is used as a treatment for prostate problems. These palms are extremely tolerant of harsh conditions, able to withstand occasional freezes, extreme drought and firestorms. In its native habitat, scorched, leafless palms will sprout new leaves after receiving ample water. The palms in this photo grow near a water feature at the Huntington Library, Art Collections, and Botanical Gardens outside Los Angeles, California.

Bottom left: The striking blue-gray color of Brahea decumbens *makes it an ideal landscape specimen for those looking for a small, spreading palm. Often used as a tall groundcover for arid gardens, this palm rarely grows taller than six feet (two meters) tall. Native to the Sierra Madre area of Mexico, this specimen grows in Southern California at the Huntington Library, Art Collections, and Botanical Gardens.*

Opposite: The blue hesper palm (Brahea armata) is a striking fan palm from Baja California. Hesper palms are extremely cold-tolerant, able to withstand severe frosts. This specimen grows near Westwood, a community in Los Angeles, California.

Following spread: The paurotis palm (Acoelorrhaphe wrightii) is native from South Florida through Central Mexico in swampy, brackish waters. Clumps spread to 15 feet (five meters) and provide a stunning tropical accent in the landscape. This photo was taken at the Gizella Kopsick Palm Arboretum in St. Petersburg, Florida, a small urban palmetum with an impressive collection of palms.

Opposite: The old man thatch palm (Coccothrinax crinata) gets its common name from the brown fibers that surround its trunk. Native to Cuba, this small palm makes an interesting conversation item in the garden. Endangered in its native habitat, this specimen was photographed at the Hawaii Tropical Botanical Garden in Hilo on the Big Island of Hawaii.

Top right: Native to Southern Florida and the Bahamas, the silver thatch palm (Coccothrinax argentata) grows in the grasslands and sand dunes throughout its range. In the landscape, this palm's glossy green and silver leaves make an outstanding display. The silver thatch palm grows to about 20 feet (seven meters) tall and is well-suited to dry, saline conditions similar to its native coastal environment.

Bottom right: Native to Cuba, Coccothrinax cupularis may be a variant of the silver thatch palm. These are excellent palms for sunny gardens in a subtropical to tropical climate. This specimen grows at the Fairchild Tropical Botanic Garden outside Miami.

Opposite: Cuban royal palms (Roystonea regia) *dwarf smaller Miraguama palms* (Coccothrinax miraguama) *at the Fairchild Tropical Botanic Garden in Miami. Both palms are native to Cuba.*

Top right: The Puerto Rico royal palm (Roystonea borinquena), *like all royal palms, makes a stunning statement as an avenue planting. Visitors to Puerto Rico or the U.S. Virgin Islands can see fine examples of this beautiful palm in its native habitat. Photo taken at the Fairchild Tropical Botanic Garden outside Miami, Florida.*

Bottom right: The Cuban royal palm (Roystonea regia) *is the most widely cultivated royal palm. In the early 19th century, thousands of Cuban royals were planted in South Florida. The Florida royal palm* (Roystonea elata) *is considered by authorities to be identical to the Cuban royal, but the Cuban royal frequently bulges in the middle of its massive gray trunk. Like other royal palms, the stunning contrast between the silvery trunk and the emerald green crownshaft makes these palms among the most sought after for the landscape market. This specimen was photographed at the Huntington Library, Art Collections, and Botanical Gardens outside Los Angeles, California.*

Following spread: A variety of palms, including several Roystonea *species, provides a stunning backdrop for a lake at the Fairchild Tropical Botanic Garden outside Miami, Florida.*

Opposite: Cuban royal palms (Roystonea regia) *are a popular choice for landscapers at exclusive resorts in tropical locations. The Grand Wailea Hotel on the Hawaiian Island of Maui is heavily landscaped with royal palms which tower over reflecting pools. Smaller pygmy date palms* (Phoenix roebelinii) *are planted in containers to accent the pool.*

Above: Tall Mexican fan palms (Washingtonia robusta) *seem to touch the heavens as they form a silhouette against the dramatic sunset of the Los Angeles sky. Los Angeles is famous for its movie industry, its exquisite sunsets and its palm-lined motorways, most of which are defined by these fan palms.*

Above: Groupings of palms, like this island in a sea of turfgrass at the Huntington Library, Art Collections, and Botanical Gardens, make an outstanding focal point. Here, needle palms (Rhapidophyllum hystrix) *form an understorey for taller Pondoland palms* (Jubaeopsis caffra). *A solitary king palm* (Archontophoenix cunninghamiana) *stands to the left. This photo also shows how palms from three continents (North America, Africa and Australia) complement each other in the landscape.*

Opposite: This mature peach palm (Bactris gasipaes) *is widely grown in its native habitat of Central and South America for its large, edible fruit. The fruit is orange when ripe and looks similar to a small peach or apricot. The trunks on these clumping palms are usually covered with spines, limiting their use in the landscape. Photographed at the McBryde Garden, part of the National Tropical Botanical Garden near Poipu Beach on the Hawaiian Island of Kauai.*

Palms of Africa and the Indian Ocean

Some of the most exotic and useful palms originate in Africa and the islands of the Indian Ocean. Because of their isolation, many island species evolved quite differently from their mainland relatives. Madagascar, the Seychelles and the Mascarene Islands are home to many rare and unusual palms that are highly prized by palm collectors and enthusiasts.

In this region, palm enthusiasts find palms which seem to walk on stilts, palms shaped like wine bottles and palms with leaves so large an entire roof could be thatched with just a few fronds.

The African continent is home to a wide diversity of palms, from the highly decorative Senegal date palms to the economically important African oil palms. In fact, the African oil palm is one of the most widely cultivated palms in the world, farmed for the rich oil its fruit produces.

This region is also home to the raffia palm, the source of fiber used to weave common twine. At 65 feet (20 meters), its leaves are among the longest of any plant in the world.

Above: Spindle palms (Hyophorbe verschaffeltii) *are an endangered species in their native habitat on the Mascarene Islands, but they are widely cultivated in subtropical and tropical locations. Named for a 19th-century nurseryman, spindle palms are tolerant of harsh conditions, including the salty air of coastal areas. They provide a distinctive accent because of their prominent waxy blue-green crownshafts and are also useful as indoor plants. This grouping was photographed in Sarasota, Florida at the Marie Selby Botanical Garden.*

Opposite: The stilt palm (Verschaffeltia splendida) *gets its common name from its stilt-like roots. Native to the steep hillsides of the Seychelle Islands, this palm is undoubtedly one of the most stunning plants in the palm group. Ideal as a solitary focal point for moist, tropical gardens, this palm deserves a place of importance in the tropical landscape. Photographed at Nani Mau Gardens outside Hilo on the Big Island of Hawaii.*

Above: An oddity in the palm world, this ilala palm (Hyphaene coriacea) *at the Foster Botanical Garden in Honolulu grows almost prostrate. In its native habitat of Madagascar and southeastern Africa, this palm reaches 30 feet (nine meters) tall and has a variety of uses. Its sap can be fermented into an alcoholic drink, and its fruit can be used as cattle fodder. The hard seeds are sometimes used as "vegetable ivory" and carved into buttons and figurines.*

Opposite: The double coconut (Lodoicea maldivica) *is a massive, impressive tree from the Seychelle Islands. In its native habitat, this tree grows to more that 80 feet (24 meters) tall with fronds that span more than 18 feet (five meters). Perhaps the most impressive feature of this tree is its large fruit, which weighs more than 45 pounds. Early Europeans thought this fruit was borne by submarine palms off the Maldive Islands, hence its Latin name. This specimen was photographed at the Foster Botanical Garden in Honolulu, Hawaii.*

Following spread: Senegal date palms (Phoenix reclinata) *make an ideal backdrop for a pond or lake. These clumping palms from Africa make outstanding landscape specimens because of their tropical appearance and easy cultural requirements. Senegal date palms are ideally suited for subtropical locations and can survive cold temperatures close to freezing. Large specimens can be seen in many comprehensive palm gardens worldwide and at tourist destinations, like Disneyland and the San Diego Zoo. Photo taken at the Fairchild Tropical Botanic Garden outside Miami, Florida. The smaller clumping palms in this photo are paurotis palms* (Acoelorrhaphe wrightii), *an American native.*

Top left: Dypsis decipiens *is a beautiful palm from Madagascar, where it grows on the high plateaus. Well-suited for the cooler tropics and subtropics, this palms deserves more attention in the landscape. This young specimen grows at the Huntington Library, Art Collections, and Botanical Gardens outside Los Angeles, California.*

Bottom left: The areca palm (Dypsis lutescens) *is one of the most common palms in cultivation, but it has become endangered in its native Madagascar because of increasing development. An outstanding palm for subtropical to tropical areas, this clumping palm can reach 35 feet (11 meters) tall, making it an ideal screen in the landscape. Its yellow, ringed trunks become more golden in full sunlight and look attractive if its stems are thinned. But the areca palm is best known as an indoor specimen and it makes an excellent house plant, provided it receives ample light and humidity. Photographed in the U.S. Virgin Islands on St. Thomas.*

Opposite: The massive palmyra palm (Borassus aethiopum) *soars to 80 feet (24 meters) tall with a trunk three feet in diameter (one meter). From the savannahs of tropical Africa, palmyra palms make an impressive statement in a large garden or park where they will dominate the landscape. This tree was photographed at the Fairchild Tropical Botanic Garden outside Miami.*

Opposite: The majesty palm (Ravenea rivularis) *gets is Latin name from "river," which describes its native habitat in Madagascar, where it grows along streambeds and in swampy areas. An attractive palm that has become popular in cultivation because of its rapid growth, the majesty palm is endangered in its native habitat. Many palm growers expected majesty palms to displace other interior palms like the areca palm and the kentia palm, but its cultural requirements, including bright lighting and consistent watering, have limited its use. Nonetheless, the majesty palm makes an attractive accent in the subtropical to tropical garden, where it typically grows to about 40 feet (12 meters) tall. Photo taken at the Huntington Library, Art Collections, and Botanical Gardens outside Los Angeles, California.*

Above: The lucubensis palm (Dyspsis madagascariensis var. lucubensis) *is native to the northern areas of Madagascar, where it grows in the dry, open forests. These palms are becoming rare in their native land because of overharvesting for palm hearts and timber. Widespread throughout the tropics, these young trees, photographed at the Huntington Library, Art Collections, and Botanical Gardens near Los Angeles, will grow to 25 feet (eight meters) tall.*

Opposite: The red latan palm (Latania lontaroides) *is native to Reunion Island in the Mascarene Island chain. Although threatened in their native land, these palms are becoming more popular in cultivation because of their stunning blue-gray fronds and relatively small size. Young palms have a reddish tinge to their leaves and leaf stalks, hence their common name. Photo taken at the Grand Wailea Hotel on the Hawaiian Island of Maui.*

Above: Growing in the shade of coconut palms (Cocos nucifera), *the Pondoland palm* (Jubaeopsis caffra) *is an attractive plant that grows to about 12 feet (four meters) tall. A unique clumping palm that is related to the coconut palm, the Pondoland palm differs greatly in its appearance and cultural requirements. The Pondoland palm grows near riverbeds in northeastern South Africa. Photographed at the Gizella Kopsick Palm Arboretum in St. Petersburg, Florida.*

Left: The long fronds of the raffia palm (Raphia farinifera) *make it a valuable palm for commerce in its native countries of Uganda, Kenya and Tanzania. Leaves are used for twine, roof thatch, brooms and baskets. Pith in the stems is ground and used as flour, and sap is fermented into an alcoholic drink. This palm was photographed at the Foster Botanical Garden in Honolulu, Hawaii.*

Opposite: The bottle palm (Hyophorbe lagenicaulis) *grows in the coastal areas and hillsides of the Mascarene Islands, where it is extremely endangered. In the landscape, bottle palms are valued for their novelty. They make an attractive focal point when planted in groups, but they make an even more dramatic statement when planted in containers. Bottle palms make excellent indoor plants, provided they receive ample light. Photo taken at the Fairchild Tropical Botanic Garden outside Miami, Florida.*

Palms of Europe and the Middle East

Some of the most useful palms in the landscape are native to Europe and the Middle East. Among them is the highly variable Mediterranean fan palm *(Chamaerops humilis)*, a staple in many palm gardens all over the world. The Mediterranean fan palm is an ideal landscape palm because of its smaller size and its ability to withstand harsh conditions, including severe drought and freezing temperatures. Variations of this palm include clumping forms, single-trunked plants, shrub-like mounds and silver blue varieties.

Another important landscape palm, the Canary Island date palm *(Phoenix canariensis)* is perhaps the finest palm for lining avenues. Indeed, the streets of Beverly Hills, California get their stately elegance from the massive Canary Island date palms that line their corridors. Native to the Canary Islands, these palms are also tolerant of drought and cold temperatures.

The true date palm *(Phoenix dactylifera)* is perhaps indigenous to Northern Africa and the Middle East, but no one knows for sure. These palms, the source of edible dates found in local markets, have been in cultivation for thousands of years. Now widespread in cultivation, date palms are among the most frequently planted landscape palms, where they are used to line roadways and parking lots in commercial areas.

Although the number of species native to Europe and the Middle East are few, their impact on civilization is enormous. Their value, practical and aesthetic, is inestimable.

Opposite: Mediterranean fan palms (Chamaerops humilis) *are among the most versatile palms in cultivation. Highly variable, these trees can grow as solitary palms, large spreading clumps or as small green mounds. Their color is equally variable, ranging from pale green to a glaucous blue. Mediterranean fan palms occur naturally in the dry areas of the Mediterranean, ranging from Portugal and Spain to Africa, Italy, France and Malta. The Mediterranean fan palm is the most northerly occurring palm, making it an ideal palm for temperate, cooler areas. This specimen was photographed at Will Rogers Park in Beverly Hills, California.*

Above: The blue gray fronds of the mazari palm (Nannorrhops ritchiana) *provide a striking contrast in the landscape. This clumping palm from the Middle East can spread to more than 20 feet (six meters), although cultivated specimens are usually much smaller. A slow grower, this palm is adapted to harsh conditions in its natural habitat, able to withstand cold climates, drought and poor, rocky soil.*

Left: The date palm (Phoenix dactylifera) *is the palm of modern commerce, planted primarily for its edible fruit. Widely cultivated for at least 5,000 years, its origin is generally considered to be the Middle East and North Africa, but botanists debate whether the date palm is a naturally occurring species or an ancient cultivated hybrid. These trees make excellent garden specimens and ideal avenue plantings. Their rapid growth, cold hardiness and drought resistance make them a landscaping staple in warm temperate locations. They look particularly attractive as poolside plantings, as this grouping at the Westin Resort on St. John in the U.S. Virgin Islands attests.*

Opposite: This cultivar of the highly variable Mediterranean fan palm (Chamaerops humilis) *is called "green mound," and it makes an ideal low-growing accent in the palm garden. This specimen grows in the palm garden at the Huntington Library, Art Collections, and Botanical Gardens near Los Angeles.*

Following spread: A stand of Canary Island date palms (Phoenix canariensis) *grow in Los Angeles outside the community of Westwood. Canary Island date palms are native to the Canary Islands and have been vital elements in the Mediterranean landscape for more than a century. All along the Riviera, thousands of Canary Island date palms were planted a century ago, giving the area its grandeur, elegance and personality. As an avenue palm, it has few rivals. Its adaptability to dry conditions, poor soil, extreme temperature shifts and salt tolerance make it one of the most important landscaping palms in cultivation. In warm temperate regions, these palms have naturalized in rocky canyons and arroyos. Visitors to Los Angeles, particularly coastal areas like Santa Monica, will view these stately palms clinging to the hillsides and palisades of the Pacific Ocean.*

Palms of Asia and Australia

Perhaps more than any other region, Asia and the South Pacific are home to some of the most diverse palms in the world. From the windmill palms of it coldest latitudes to the sealing wax palms of the steamy jungles, the region is home to the most exotic and colorful palms in the world.

Among these is the strikingly exotic sealing wax palm *(Cyrtostachys renda)*. With its flaming red crownshaft, this palm makes an indelible impression on anyone who has seen one. These palms are truly exotic and adaptable only to the warmest, most humid areas of the world.

Throughout Asia, fishtail palms, with their odd-shaped leaves, make a striking impact. Aptly named because their leaves look like jagged fish tails, these palms are fast growers and make stunning accompaniments to palm gardens around the world.

Not only decorative, the palms of Asia and the South Pacific have economic importance for the various goods they produce. Seeds of some are carved into buttons and figurines and used as vegetable ivory. The fruit of others, like the betel nut palm, is used as a mild narcotic or stimulant, and rattan is harvested from the trunks of others and fashioned into furniture. Oddities in the palm world, rattan palms climb like vines through the forests, hooking themselves to other trees with sharp claws that grow from their stems or leaves.

Opposite: The Livistona *genus contains many species that are widely grown worldwide. In this photo, three species* (Livistona chinensis, saribus, decipiens) *make a stunning focal point by the lake at the Fairchild Tropical Botanic Garden outside Miami, Florida.*

Above: Areca vestiara *is a dramatic, attractive clumping palm from Sulawesi, Celebes and the Moluccas. This palm grows atop stilt roots to 20 feet (six meters) tall. Becoming popular in cultivation because of its brilliant orange or red crownshaft, this palm deserves a place of prominence in the tropical landscape. Photographed at the Hoomaluhia Botanical Garden in Kaneohe on the Hawaiian Island of Oahu.*

Above: Pygmy date palms (Phoenix roebelinii) *are ideal palms for the small garden. Rarely exceeding 12 feet (four meters) tall, these palms are among the most versatile for the subtropical and tropical gardens. As small plants, pygmy date palms make ideal container plants for bright interiors. Mature specimens make a stunning display in the garden, particularly when grouped in an island, as they are in this display at the Huntington Library, Art Collections, and Botanical Gardens near Los Angeles, California. Native to Laos, pygmy date palms can be found in nearly every tropical region.*

Opposite: Members of the Phoenix *genus hybridize freely, and many trees which are sold as pure species are actually hybrids. The parentage of this hybrid at the Huntington Library, Art Collections, and Botanical Gardens is unknown, but it appears to be a hybrid between a pygmy date palm* (Phoenix roebellini) *and another species.*

Opposite: The Ceylon date palm (Phoenix loureiroi) *is native to India and Sri Lanka. A small, slow-growing palm, the Ceylon date palm makes a beautiful statement with its slender trunk covered with spiny leaf bases. Hardy to temperatures below freezing, this palm is an ideal landscape specimen for sunny locations in temperate and tropical climates. This palm grows in the Huntington Library, Art Collections, and Botanical Gardens outside Los Angeles, California.*

Above: Taller, but similar to the pygmy date palm, the elegant cliff date palm (Phoenix rupicola) *deserves more attention from landscapers. Native to India, these palms have glossy green leaves and a tropical appearance, but they grow equally well in cooler subtropical regions. Here, a mature specimen grows at the Gizella Kopsick Palmetum in St. Petersburg, Florida, surrounded by palms from around the world, including a clumping Mediterranean fan palm* (Chamaerops humilis) *in the foreground.*

Following spread: This palm glade is truly stunning and includes a variety of palms such as betel nut palms (Areca catechu). *Native to Southeast Asia, betel nut palms have glossy green leaves and a prominent green crownshaft. Attractive landscape palms, betel nut palms are commonly grown for their seeds, which are used as a stimulant. Amidst the betel nut palms, sealing wax palms* (Cyrtostachys renda) *display their stunning red trunks. Native to the swampforests of Thailand, Malaysia and Indonesia, sealing wax palms are considered by many to be the most beautiful palms in the world. Sealing wax palms are so named because their bright red crownshafts are similar in shade to the wax used by colonial British to seal their letters. Smaller* Licuala *palms, with fronds that resemble large hands, appear in the foreground. Photographed at the Hoomaluhia Botanical Garden in Kaneohe on the Hawaiian Island of Oahu.*

Left: The windmill palm (Trachycarpus fortunei) is one of the most cold-hardy species of palms. Native to China, these slow-growing palms have fan-shaped leaves and fiber-covered trunks, making them interesting conversation pieces in the garden. Able to withstand snow and temperatures well below freezing, these palms can be grown in cold-temperate regions of the world, provided they receive full sun and some winter protection. This specimen grows at the Los Angeles Arboretum and Botanic Garden in California.

Opposite: From India and Pakistan, the silver date palm (Phoenix sylvestris) is similar in appearance to the Canary Island date palm, but its fronds are distinctly silver blue. A stunning palm for subtropical and tropical areas, the silver date palm is easy to grow and provides a nice focal point for a large garden. Photo taken at the Huntington Library, Art Collections, and Botanical Gardens outside Los Angeles.

Top: This photo demonstrates the beauty landscapers can create in a palm-only garden. Palms from around the world complement each other nicely, showing the high degree of variability in this remarkable family of plants. In the center of the photo, a Livistona *palm stands like a sentinel over smaller-growing species. Photo taken at the Huntington Library, Art Collections, and Botanical Gardens outside Los Angeles, California.*

Opposite: From the Ryukyu Islands of Japan, the satake palm (Satakentia liukiuensis) *provides an elegant focal point in the garden. With its arching leaves, graceful trunk and purplish crownshaft, satake palms can be grown in warm temperate regions, although this specimen grows in a distinctly tropical environment at the National Botanical Garden on Kauai in the Hawaiian Islands.*

Following spread: Chinese fan palms (Livistona chinensis) *are natives of Japan and Taiwan, but they are grown worldwide in warm temperate to tropical locations. Mature Chinese fan palms look attractive planted in alleys, as evidenced in this avenue planting at the Fairchild Tropical Botanic Garden outside Miami, Florida.*

Left: Sun illuminates the unique leaves of the mountain fishtail palm (Caryota gigas). Native to Thailand, Laos and China, these trees grows rapidly to a massive size. With their long, exotic fronds, fishtail palms add a startling contrast in the landscape. Like all single-trunked fishtail palms, mountain fishtail palms will die after producing seed upon reaching maturity. Photo taken at the Huntington Library, Art Collections, and Botanical Gardens near Los Angeles, California.

Opposite: From the Vanuatu archipelago and the Solomon Islands, Metroxylon warburgii grows in the rainforests and the swamps at low elevations. Growing to 25 feet (8 meters) tall, this beautiful palm has strongly arched fronds which are 10 feet (3 meters) long. This grove grows at the Hoomaluhia Botanical Garden in Kaneohe on the Hawaiian Island of Oahu.

Following spread: Palm trees make ideal avenue plantings, particularly when a single species is used. These Australian fan palms (Livistona australis) add grace and elegance to the former estate of Henry Huntington, now the Huntington Library, Art Collections, and Botanical Gardens outside Los Angeles, California.

Opposite: The sealing wax palm (Cyrtostachys renda) *is one of the most striking species of palms. Native to the humid tropics of Thailand, Indonesia and Malaysia, this beautiful palm gets its common name from the brilliant red color of its trunk, nearly a match for the red wax used to seal envelopes during British colonial times. Many palm enthusiasts outside of the tropics have sought to grow them, but these palms require warm, humid conditions to survive. This specimen grows in Kailua-Kona on the Big Island of Hawaii.*

Right: From New Guinea, Hydriastele microspadix *forms an attractive clump that looks similar to bamboo. The trunks on this palm appear slightly purple, making them attractive specimen palms for the wet tropics. Photo taken at the Fairchild Tropical Botanic Garden near Miami, Florida.*

Opposite: Massed together, these king palms (Archontophoenix cunninghamiana) *make a stunning focal point at the Huntington Library, Art Collections, and Botanical Gardens near Los Angeles. Masses of clivias thrive in the shade of these mature trees. Native to Australia, king palms, with their ringed, grey trunks and green crownshafts, are among the most tropical-looking palms for cooler subtropical areas, and are able to withstand occasional frosts. Relatively fast growing and easy to maintain, king palms are among the most commonly planted palms in Southern California.*

Right: King palms make excellent avenue palms, as evidenced in this photo from the Los Angeles suburb of Westwood. The bright red fruit of these palms provides seasonal interest.

119

Left: The amethyst flowers of the king palm (Archontophoenix cunninghamiana) *provide an attractive accent in the subtropical garden. Photographed at Will Rogers Park on Sunset Boulevard in Beverly Hills, California.*

Opposite: The Mount Lewis palm (Archontophoenix purpurea) *is distinguished by its purplish crownshaft. Native to Queensland, Australia where it grows at 4,000 feet (1,219 meters), this attractive palm is beginning to gain popularity as a landscape specimen. This young tree grows at the Fairchild Tropical Botanic Garden near Miami, Florida.*

Opposite: Naturalized on the north coast of the Big Island of Hawaii, Alexander palms (Archontophoenix alexandrae) grow rapidly near streambeds in the valleys and ravines that define the area. This photo was taken just east of Hilo on the Big Island of Hawaii.

Right: Hyphaene dichotoma *is an oddity in the palm world, a palm with a branching trunk. This genus is native to India, Africa and the Middle East, where its hard seeds are used as "vegetable ivory," carved into figurines and buttons. Photo taken at the Fairchild Tropical Botanic Garden outside Miami, Florida.*

Opposite: The Pritchardia *genus includes about 30 species from the South Pacific, many of which are native to the Hawaiian Islands. Called loulou palms, these palms are the only true natives of Hawaii. Coconut palms* (Cocos nucifera) *may have been introduced by early inhabitants from the Marquesas Islands or Tahiti. Named for Sir John Thurston, a 19th-century governor of Fiji, the Thurston palm* (Pritchardia thurstonii) *is one of the most beautiful in the genus. Photo taken at the Hoomaluhia Botanical Garden in Kaneohe on the Hawaiian Island of Oahu.*

Right: Native to the Big Island of Hawaii, Pritchardia affinis *is probably extinct in the wild, but it is widely grown as a landscape palm because of its distinctive wedge-shaped fronds. The Foster Botanical Garden in Honolulu houses a fine collection of loulou palms, including the specimen in this photo.*

Top left: Pritchardia remota *is now endangered in its habitat on the Hawaiian Island of Nihoa. This palm grows at the Foster Botanical Garden in Honolulu.*

Bottom left: Also from Hawaii, Pritchardia lowreyana *is a medium-sized palm that inhabits moist forest areas. A good landscaping plant that benefits from a sunny but sheltered position, it also makes a useful container plant if a large container is used.* Pritchardia lowreyana *is native to the island of Molokai. This specimen at the Foster Botanical Garden in Honolulu, on the Hawaiian Island of Oahu, is registered as an "exceptional tree" in Hawaii.*

*Opposite: The Fiji fan palm (*Pritchardia pacifica*) probably originated in Tonga but was introduced to Fiji centuries ago. Now widely cultivated in tropical regions, these palms are ideal for coastal areas, where they can withstand ocean spray. In Fiji, the fronds of this majestic palm were used to make fans for tribal leaders. Photographed at the National Tropical Botanical Garden on Kauai in the Hawaiian Islands.*

Following spread: Pritchardia arecina *is a mid-sized palm that grows in the rainforest areas on the Hawaiian Island of Maui, typically on the eastern end of the island in the wet, mountainous areas. Visitors to Maui frequently pass through its native habitat on the "Road to Hana," a popular tourist destination. This photo was taken in its native area outside Hana at the Piilanihale Heiau, a focal point of Kahanu Gardens. This "heiau," or "temple," was built by the Piilani dynasty in the 14th century and had been hidden by Hawaii's dense jungles for centuries. In the 1970s, the overgrowth was cleared, revealing a structure that covered nearly three acres. Kahanu Gardens is landscaped with many native Hawaiian plants, including* Pritchardia *palms.*

Opposite: From the coastal areas and lowland forests of Vanuatu, the Montgomery palm (Veitchia arecina) is gaining popularity as a landscape palm. With its tall, slender trunk and arching fronds, this palm makes a graceful impression to the tropical garden. Photographed at the National Tropical Botanical Garden on Kauai in the Hawaiian Islands.

Top left: The Montgomery palm (Veitchia arecina) is one of the most cold tolerant of the genus, able to grow in warmer subtropical areas. This palm is named for Colonel Robert Montgomery, founder of the Fairchild Tropical Botanic Garden. Photo taken at the Fairchild Tropical Botanic Garden near Miami, Florida.

Bottom right: The Fairchild Tropical Botanic Garden near Miami, Florida has an excellent collection of Veitchii palms. Veitchii winin is also from Vanuatu and is similar to the Montgomery palm.

Following spread: The Koolau Mountains on the Hawaiian Island of Oahu provide a stunning backdrop for these Areca triandra palms. In the distance, fishtail palms (Caryota species) provide an interesting contrast. Photo taken at the Hoomaluhia Botanical Garden in Kaneohe on the Hawaiian Island of Oahu.

Left: The shaving brush palm (Rhopalostylis sapida) gets its common name from its bulging crownshaft and upright fronds, which make it look like a large shaving brush in the landscape. Also called the nikau palm, this tree is native to the cool, damp forests of New Zealand and the Chatham Islands and has the distinction of being the world's southernmost occurring species. In its native habitat, this palm has several uses. Indigenous Maoris fell the trees for the edible cabbage. The fronds are also used for thatching roofs. The specimen in this photo grows in the subtropical climate of the Huntington Library, Art Collections, and Botanical Gardens outside Los Angeles, California.

Opposite: The Livistona *genus includes about 34 species of palms which range from the Old World through the South Pacific. The Australian fan palm (*Livistona australis*) is among the most commonly grown in warm temperate regions. Native to the east coast of Australia where it grows in the rainforests, this palm grows well in cooler climates and can withstand frosts. The Australian fan palm is the second most southernly growing species, second only to the shaving brush palm. Photo taken in one of the formal gardens of the Huntington Library, Art Collections, and Botanical Gardens outside Los Angeles.*

Opposite: The ruffled fan palm (Licuala grandis) *grows in the rainforests of Vanuatu and the Solomon Islands. One of most attractive species in the palm family, these trees are sought and planted by palm collectors around the world. Rarely reaching more than 10 feet (three meters) tall, this tree makes an ideal understorey subject for the tropics, as one can see from this tree growing under an oak tree at Fairchild Tropical Botanic Garden outside Miami, Florida.*

Top right: The Manila palm (Adonidia merrillii) *is one of the most common palms in the Philippines and is a popular landscape palm in tropical areas. These trees are easy to grow and are frequently used by interiorscape designers in shopping malls and office buildings. It is also called the Christmas palm because of its bright red fruit produced around Christmas in areas north of the equator. Unfortunately, these beautiful palms are highly susceptible to the lethal yellowing disease, which has decimated most mature specimens in South Florida and the Caribbean. This grouping grows at the Westin Resort on St. John in the U.S. Virgin Islands.*

Bottom right: The wet rainforests of Samoa are home to Clinostigma samoense. *With its green and white ringed trunk and lime green crownshaft, this palm is stunning in the landscape. This palm is suited to wet, humid tropical climates. An ideal addition to any collection,* Clinostigma samoense *is grown in many botanical gardens, including the Hoomaluhia Botanical Garden in Kaneohe on the Hawaiian Island of Oahu.*

Public Gardens

Below is a list of gardens that have excellent palm collections. At many of these locations, you can view the palms that were photographed for this book.

UNITED STATES

Fairchild Tropical Botanic Garden
10901 Old Cutler Road
Coral Gables (Miami), FL 33156
(305) 667-1651
http://www.fairchildgarden.org

Foster Botanical Garden
50 North Vineyard Boulevard
Honolulu, Hawaii 96817
(808) 522-7066
http://www.co.honolulu.hi.us/parks/
hbg/fbg.htm

Fullerton Arboretum
1900 Associated Road
Fullerton, CA 92831
(714) 278-3579
http://www.arboretum.fullerton.edu

Gizella Kopsick Palm Arboretum
North Shore Drive
St. Petersburg, FL
727) 893-7335
http://www.stpete.org/palm.htm

Hawaii Tropical Botanical Garden
27-717 Old Mamalahoa Highway
Papaikou, HI 96781
808-964-5233
http://www.htbg.com

Hoomaluhia Botanical Garden
45-680 Luluku Road
Kaneohe, HI 96744
Phone: (808) 233-7323
http://www.co.honolulu.hi.us/parks/
hbg/hmbg.htm

Huntington Library, Art
Collections, & Botanical Gardens
1151 Oxford Road
San Marino (Los Angeles), CA
91108
(626) 405-2100
http://www.huntington.org

Koko Crater Botanical Garden
Inside Koko Crater
Honolulu, HI 96825
(808) 522-7060
http://www.co.honolulu.hi.us/parks/
hbg/kcbg.htm

Los Angeles County Arboretum
& Botanic Garden
301 N. Baldwin Avenue
Arcadia, CA 91007
(626) 821-3222
http://www.arboretum.org

Lotusland
695 Ashley Road
Santa Barbara, CA 93108
(805) 969-9990
http://www.lotusland.org

Marie Selby Botanical Garden
811 South Palm Avenue
Sarasota, FL 34236
(941) 366-5731
http://www.selby.org

Mildred E. Mathias Botanical
Garden
University of California, Los Angeles
Los Angeles, CA 90095
310-825-1260
http://www.botgard.ucla.edu/

Myakka River State Park
13207 S.R. 72
Sarasota, FL 34241
(941) 361-6511
http://www.floridastateparks.org/
myakkariver/default.asp

Nani Mau Gardens
421 Makalika Street
Hilo, HI 96720
(808) 959-3500
http://www.nanimau.com

National Tropical Botanical Garden
3530 Papalina Road
Kalaheo, HI 96741
(808) 332-7324
Locations throughout Hawaii
http://ntbg.org/

Palm Canyon
Palm Springs, CA
(800) 790-3398
http://www.palmsprings.com/points/
canyon/index.html

Quail Botanical Gardens
230 Quail Gardens Drive
Encinitas, CA 92024
(760) 436-3036
http://www.qbgardens.org

San Diego Zoo
2920 Zoo Drive
San Diego, CA 92100
(619) 234-3153
http://www.sandiegozoo.org

Virginia Robinson Gardens
Beverly Hills, CA 90210
(310) 276-5367
http://parks.co.la.ca.us/
virginia_gardens.html

Wahiawa Botanical Garden
1396 California Avenue
Wahiawa, HI 96786
Phone: (808) 621-7321
http://www.co.honolulu.hi.us/parks/
hbg/wbg.htm

World Botanical Gardens
19 Mile Marker, Highway 19
Umauma, HI
http://www.wbgi.com

AUSTRALIA

Brisbane Botanic Gardens
Mt Coot-tha Road
Brisbane, Queensland
07 3403 8888
http://www.brisbane.qld.gov.au/
community/facilities/parks/
botanic_gardens.shtml

ENGLAND

Royal Botanic Gardens, Kew
Richmond, Surrey TW9 2AB
020 8332 5655
http://www.rbgkew.org.uk

The Hawaii Tropical Botanical Garden near Hilo has an impressive collection of tropical plants. Overlooking the Pacific Ocean, this garden was carved out of an overgrown jungle and now includes a fine collection of palms, including this stand of Alexander palms (Archontophoenix alexandrae), *native to Australia.*

Acknowledgements

I could fill an entire chapter with the names of those who have helped me with this project. Members of the International Palm Society, photographers and fellow authors helped shape the book you are holding.

I'd particularly like to thank Tammy Guerra, publication manager, for her enthusiam and hard work. Working with Tammy is a sheer pleasure.

Don Hodel, one of the world's leading authorities on palms and author of several outstanding palm books, provided invaluable help. Don reviewed and corrected the scientific names of the palms in this book.

On the production side, photographer Patrick Gee taught me how to make the palm trees I see in the landscape come alive on film. Dan Poynter of Para Publishing deserves my gratitude for imparting his vast knowledge of the publishing industry. Dan Margulis, one of the nation's leading pre-press authorities, taught me the pre-press techniques I needed to complete this project.

Lee Varis prepared the photos in this book for press. Lee is one of the top digital imaging professionals in the world, and I'm grateful he lives in my hometown of Los Angeles, California.

Special thanks to Sabra Chili and the staff at Daehan Printing for moving my ideas into production.

Robert Davies, renowned Florida landscape architect, is a fellow palm lover. Robert helped me identify several outstanding palm gardens in Florida.

Members of the International Palm Society encouraged me to publish this book. The International Palm Society provided me with a wealth of information about the palms I photographed.

I must also thank, most sincerely, my family and friends for their support and encouragement. Terrance Leaser helped me select photo sites and assisted me on photo shoots. Mark Leaser provided constant encouragement and technical expertise. Emi Harnden, Matt Ingebrigtsen, Bob Redpath and Heidi Wulkow provided great ideas and inspiration. And I cannot forget Rusty, my four-legged shadow, truly man's best friend.

Resources

Barrow, Sasha. 1998. *A Revision of Phoenix.* London. Reprinted from *Kew Bulletin* 53 (3).

Broschat, Timothy K., and Alan W. Meerow. 2000. *Ornamental Palm Horticulture.* Gainesville, Florida: University Press of Florida.

Dransfield, John, and Henk Beentje. 1995. *The Palms of Madagascar.* London: Board of Trustees of the Royal Botanic Gardens: Kew.

Ellison, Don, and Anthony Ellison. 2001. *Betrock's Cultivated Palms of the World.* Hollywood, Florida: Betrock Information Systems.

Gibbons, Martin. 1993. *Palms.* Seacaucus, New Jersey: Chartwell Books.

Henderson, Andrew, Gloria Galeano, and Rodrigo Bernal. 1995. *Palms of the Americas.* Princeton, New Jersey: Princeton University Press.

Hodel, Donald R., ed. 1998. *The Palms and Cycads of Thailand.* Lawrence, Kansas: Allen Press.

Hodel, Donald R. 1992. *Chamaedorea Palms: The Species and their Cultivation.* Lawrence, Kansas: Allen Press.

Jones, David L. 1995. *Palms Throughout the World.* Washington, D.C.: Smithsonian Institution Press.

Meerow, Alan W. 1992. *Betrock's Guide to Landscape Palms.* Cooper City, Florida: Betrock Information Systems.

Osborn, B., T. Reynoso & G. Stein. 2000. *Palms for Southern California – A Quick Reference Guide to Palms. Third Edition.* The Palm Society of Southern California.

Principes (later *Palms*). 1956-2003. Journal of the International Palm Society, Lawrence, Kansas. Vols. 1-45.

Romney, David H. 1997. *Growing Coconuts in South Florida.* Homestead, Florida: David H. Romney.

Sunset. 2001. *Western Garden Book.* Menlo Park, California: Sunset Publishing Corp.

Uhl, Natalie W., and John Dransfield. 1987. *Genera Palmarum.* Lawrence, Kansas: L.H. Bailey Hortorium and International Palm Society.

Warren, William. 1997. *The Tropical Garden.* New York, New York: Thames and Hudson, Inc.

Index